GULF OF MEXICO

CANCUN

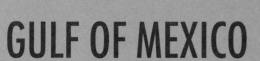

NORTHERN YUCATAN

Chichen Itza

Uxmal

Tulum

Labnah

Edzna

Becan

Chicanna

Kohunlich

SOUTHERN YUCATAN

Palenque

Tikal

BELIZE

GULF OF HONDURAS

GUATEMALA

HONDURAS

VAL BRINKERHOFF AND JOSEPH L. ALLEN

VISUALIZING

THE LANDS OF THE

BOOK OF MORMON

Published by Covenant Communications, Inc., American Fork, Utah
Copyright © 2007
Photographs © Val Brinkerhoff (except where noted)
Text © Joseph L. Allen

Printed in Mexico
First Printing: October 2007

14 13 12 11 10 09 08 07   10 9 8 7 6 5 4 3 2 1

ISBN-13 978-1-59811-403-4
ISBN-10 1-59811-403-4

VISUALIZING
THE LANDS OF THE
BOOK OF MORMON

VAL BRINKERHOFF AND JOSEPH L. ALLEN

© Chris Parkinson

No work is created in isolation. I would like to thank Joseph L. Allen for his insightful commentary on the culture, people, and ruins associated with these photographs. His understanding of the sites and events connected to them in relationship to the Book of Mormon adds essential context to what is seen. I would also like to thank the Visual Arts Department, the College of Fine Arts and Communications, the Office of Research and Creative Activity, BYU Travel Study, and many supportive people at Brigham Young University for their continuing support of this and other research efforts in various parts of the world, all of it centering on sacred architecture and what it can teach us. I express gratitude for the assistance of Margaret Weber, Kathryn Jenkins, Kirk Shaw, and others at Covenant Communications for this opportunity to share photographs from a number of these travels. I have been fortunate to experience many of these special places with my students and friends. Their insights and help has been key to success. Lastly, without the patient support of my wife, Trina, and our children, this work would not exist.

—Val Brinkerhoff

CONTENTS

INTRODUCTION

Architecture is fundamental to existence and can serve as an important conduit to the sacred. It is the art form that encompasses all others. The world's most spectacular human creations are temples built to honor and worship God and kings. Speaking of architecture as a whole, John Lane said, "Architecture is the one art which affects us all. People can choose not to listen to music or to look at sculpture, to visit theatres and cinemas, but the buildings around us shape everyone's world."

Exchanging the tension, noise, and complexity of the modern world for the solitude of mysterious stones in ancient America provides us with time to ponder and meditate. Sitting high atop a massive pyramid temple in the jungle of Central America allows deep meaning to be gleaned from deep reflection.

What is it that motivated ancient American cultures to create the marvels at Tikal, Palenque, Chichen Izta, and Machu Picchu? In those locations, incredible feats of engineering and artistry work together to form curious temples constructed to worship God, honor kings, and symbolize the mysteries of the cosmos. For centuries sacred architecture has emerged in the deserts and jungles of this promised land, signaling the rise and fall of peoples who combined art and religion into grand monuments of stone. Who were they? How did they worship? Why did they disappear? The Book of Mormon holds many answers.

The magnificence, beauty, and curiosity of these impressive temples have attracted pilgrims for centuries, many of them seeking peace and enlightenment. Today freedom from cell phones, media, and stress provides additional motivation to visit those sites. Those familiar with the rewards of the ancient world seek solitude, rejuvenation, even revelation in their visits. Yet for many, it is the art, architecture, or engineering that makes these sacred places attractive, along with the unique cultures, landscapes, and native peoples that surround them. For many people, the promise of new insights and understanding easily overcomes the oppressive heat and humidity, large insects, and significant travel expenses.

This is especially true for Latter-day Saints who yearn for greater understanding of the people and events connected to Book of Mormon lands: the people who were baptized at the Waters of Mormon, those who heard Samuel the Lamanite's call to repentance high atop ancient stone walls, and those who fought alongside Moroni, defending family, home, and temple. Many desire to experience these sacred sites firsthand, hoping to feel the spirit of these places and their people from the unique Book of Mormon perspective.

(Right)
Tula, West Central Mexico

(Above-left)
Teotihuacan, Mexico

(Above-right)
Uxmal, Mexico

(Right)
Palenque, Mexico

(Right)
Tikal, Guatemala

(Left)
Coast of Veracruz, Mexico

(Right)
Palenque, Mexico

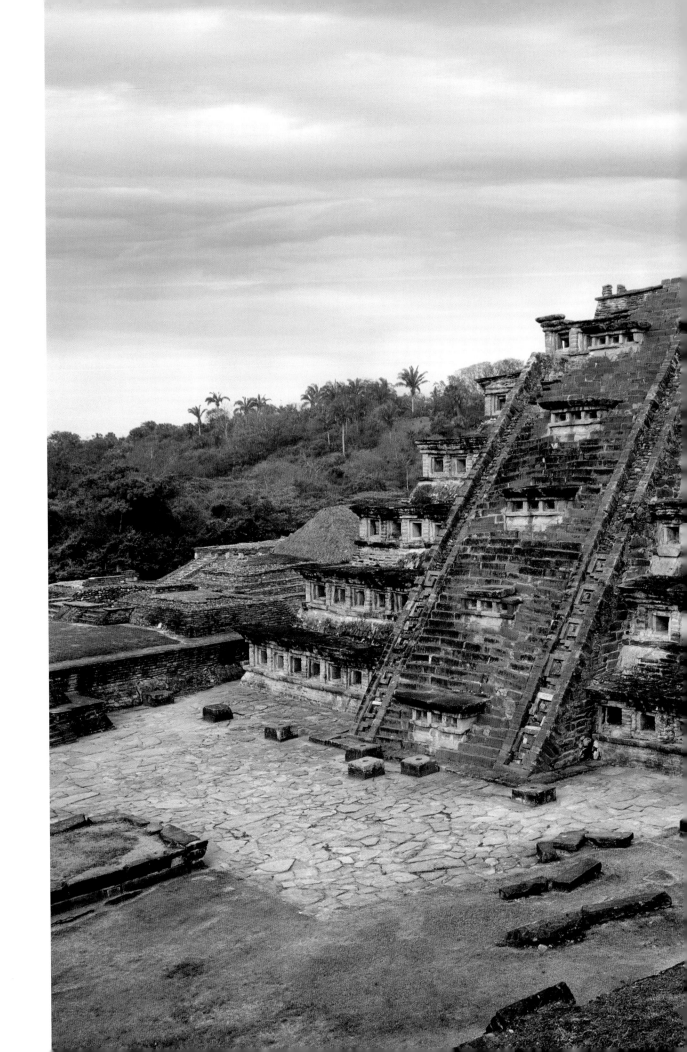

(Left)
El Tajin, Mexico

For a temple-centered people, the profound beauty and incredible skill evidenced at these ancient temple sites, along with the deep sense of history, reverence, and curiosity surrounding them, combine to both delight and perplex. The experience can be exhilarating, inviting continuous exploration of more ruins.

Like those of the Egyptians of the Old World, the architecture and art of ancient Americans were highly visual, full of religious and cultural concepts normally taught only within the confines of sacred spaces. These spaces reveal many archetypal patterns, using the consistent proportions and inspired forms that pervade much of sacred architecture worldwide—even of widely divergent faiths and cultures. These archetypal patterns are found in the geometry, in the orientation in space, and in the use of evocative art, decorative motifs, and architectural forms, all symbolizing the culture's most important truths.

For sensitive Latter-day Saints, sacred architecture is of eternal importance. Temples are the sacred schools in which we are taught eternal truths about God and the ultimate potential and destiny of His children. Joseph Smith's primary mission in restoring the gospel was to bring back the priesthood, which holds the keys to the saving and exalting ordinances of the temple, thus giving man the opportunity to again dwell in God's presence. The Book of Mormon was the first means of reintroducing these truths to our dispensation. The stories and lessons throughout its ancient pages provide lessons for modern man. These often center on pride and materialism and the resulting fall of entire civilizations.

(Left)
Edzna, Mexico

While marveling at the majesty of these ancient structures, one is also humbled by their demise, mindful that the glory of any civilization is not in its architecture but in the full development of its people.

TEOTIHUACAN

Before there was light
Before there was day
When there was still darkness
The gods met in council in TEOTIHUACAN
(Florentine Codex, AD 1566)

In the Nauhtl (Aztec) language, the word for god is Teo. The interpretation of *Teotihuacan* (tay-oh-tee-wah'kahn) is "the pathway that leads to the city of the gods."

Now archaeological ruins, the city-state of Teotihuacan, which is located 7000 feet above sea level in the sprawling Mexico valley and about 25 miles northeast of Mexico City, endured for more than a millennium from about 200 BC to AD 800. For six hundred years (200 BC to AD 400) it was contemporary with the Nephite history. At AD 400, shortly after the demise of the Nephite nation, Teotihuacan may have been the largest city in the world, supporting a population of an estimated 150,000 inhabitants.

The downfall of Teotihuacan appears to have resulted from a society built upon secret combinations. Dr. Ignacio Bernal wrote that "the primary reason for the decline and fall of Teotihuacan was the excessive centralization of the major powers of the society—that is, the combination of the merchants, priests and military."

Teotihuacan appears also to have played a major role in the downfall of the Nephite nation. Mormon wrote, "And behold, in the end of this book ye shall see that this Gadianton did prove the overthrow, yea, almost the entire destruction of the people of Nephi. Behold I do not mean the end of the book of Helaman, but I mean the end of the book of Nephi, from which I have taken all the account which I have written" (Helaman 2:13–14).

Teotihuacan's contact with the Nephite society appears to have been as early as 46 BC, when as a result of "much contention and many dissensions . . . an exceedingly great many . . . departed out of the land of Zarahemla, and went forth unto the land northward to inherit the land" (Helaman 3:3). Teotihuacan is proposed as the area referred to as the land northward, an area consisting of large bodies of water, an area of a small amount of timber, and an area where the people became expert in the workings of cement (see Helaman 3:4–7).

Teotihuacan appears to fit the above requirements, and there is archaeological evidence that it was an ethnically diverse city with distinct Zapotec and Mayan

(Previous Page)
The serpent played a major role as the primary deity in Mesoamerican culture. The serpent also figures in both the Bible and the Book of Mormon as a type and shadow of Christ. The apostate representation of deity displayed on the temple of Quetzalcoatl at Teotihuacan was indeed impressive as its eyes were originally inset with beautiful black obsidian stones and the buildings were painted a vibrant deep red color.

(Right)
This elaborately designed stone called the Aztec Calendar Stone, also known as the Sun Stone, is twelve feet in diameter, three feet thick, and weighs about twenty-four tons. Today it is located at the back of the Aztec room of the National Museum of Anthropology and History in Mexico City. It is not designed to be a functional calendar but rather to depict the structure of the fifty-two-year calendar cycle. It shows the twenty named days and the thirteen named months of the Aztec calendar along with the five extra days required to reach the 365-day solar year. It also illustrates the four earth destructive periods associated with water, wind, earth, and fire.

quarters as early as 50 BC, indicating migrations from the Tehuantepec (land of Zarahemla) region.

At about 30 BC, a secret combination made a man named Jacob their leader. They fled from the land southward to the "northernmost part of the land" (proposed Teotihuacan), where they proceeded to "build up unto themselves a kingdom" (3 Nephi 7:12; see also 3 Nephi 7:9–13; 9:9).

On May 4, AD 374, a dictator from Teotihuacan referred to as Spearthrower Owl, and who appears to have been a descendant of the Jacobian dynasty, ascended to the throne at Teotihuacan. His activities apparently led to the complete destruction of the Nephite nation.

(Previous Page)
A picture of the Pyramid of the Sun showing mountains in the background. The pyramid was extensively excavated in the first decade of the twentieth century by Leopordo Batres. Since that time, two tunnels have been excavated into the core of the pyramid, providing more information about its chronology and substructure. Another extensive excavation by INAH (Instituto Nacional de Antropología e Historia), directed by Eduardo Matos Moctezuma in 1992–93, exposed more of the pyramid complex. Although no tombs have been found inside the structure, a cave was discovered which may suggest a ritualistic reason for building on that spot.

(Above)
The all-seeing eye is a symbol of many cultures and is reflected among the buildings of Teotihuacan.

(Right)
One of several serpent-bird motifs located on the temple of Quetzalcoatl at Teotihuacan. Dating to AD 200–300, the artwork is indicative of the Classic period in Mesoamerica. It helps explain what the Book of Mormon is referring to regarding that same time period: "And they did still continue to build up churches unto themselves, and adorn them with all manner of precious things. And thus did two hundred and fifty years pass away" (4 Nephi 1:41).

The quetzal bird-and-serpent motif is a perpetual theme in both history and architecture throughout Mesoamerica. At Teotihuacan, legend reports that Quetzalcoatl was creator of the universe and that he traveled across the earth gathering together the bones of the deceased. The different representations of this theme are portrayed by the lavishly arrayed man with a headdress of quetzal bird feathers holding a serpent in his hand (lower-left and bottom-center) and the motif of a serpent with feathers extending from the face (lower-right). Creation and death themes are illustrated in the two upper-left photographs.

(Right)
These tombs at Teotihuacan are duplicated in other parts of Mesoamerica by individual people. It is traditional for people to imitate or build after the style of the hierarchy. Most Mesoamerican cultures maintained a strong commitment to life after death, a belief reflected in their tombs. Even today, it is important for the people in Mexico to be buried inside or near a religious shrine.

(Left)

The ruins of Tula are located about an hour and a half north of Mexico City, near the town of San Marcos. Tula bridges the historical gap between the ruins of Teotihuacan and the Aztec center of Tenochtitlan, dating from AD 900 to 1200. The Toltec civilization's major city was Tula, which means "abundance" or "bountiful." The Toltec people worshiped the white god Quetzalcoatl. LDS scholars have wondered about Tula's people, but it is unlikely the city is that of Bountiful from the Book of Mormon. However, the large soldier monuments and serpent motifs proclaimed it to be a major city center. It is considered the birth place of the tenth-century warrior named Topiltzin Quetzalcoatl, who had bestowed upon himself the deified name Quetzalcoatl. To-piltzin is reported to have been driven out of the Mexico valley, afterward promising to return. Tradition suggests that he then traveled to the Yucatan and gained control over the Mayan city of Chichen Itza. The temple of Kukulcan (Quetzalcoatl) at Chichen Itza was built over a Mayan temple and dates from AD 1000 to 1200.

(Above)

It has been stated that in all of America's past, no figure is more mysterious and more frustrating than the fair god Quetzalcoatl, who was born of a virgin, came from the east, died, resurrected, and promised to return to his people. The sixteenth-century conquering Catholic priests scoffed at the concept of a white god and claimed Quetzalcoatl was of the devil. At Teotihuacan, the stone feather serpent was developed before Christ's birth and was prominent during the Toltec, Mayan, and Aztec eras.

(Right)

A view of the Pyramid of the Sun at night. A sixteenth-century Franciscan monk named Bernardino de Sahagun wrote: "It is told that when yet all was darkness, when yet no sun had shone and no dawn had broken—it is said—the gods gathered themselves there at Teotihuacan. They spoke; they said among themselves: Come hither, O gods! Who will carry the burden? Who will take it upon himself to be the sun, to bring the dawn?"

COAST OF VERACRUZ

At the entrance of the Olmec Museum at Jalapa, Veracruz, Mexico, the following words are written:

People of Mexico, give heed:
This is the beginning of your history,
your cradle and your altar.
Listen to the silent voices of Mexico's oldest culture,
Perhaps the mother civilization of our continent.

The Olmecs converted the rain into harvests,
The sun into the calendar.
The rocks into scripture,
The cotton into clothing.

Travels into commerce,
Mounds into thrones.
Jaguars into religion,
And men into Gods.

Agustin Acosta Lagunes, November 1986

In the early part of the 4th century BC, Moroni, the son of Mormon, wrote, "And now I, Moroni, proceed to give an account of those

Bottom center, pyramid at night © Matthew Turley

ancient inhabitants who were destroyed by the hand of the Lord upon the face of this north country" (Ether 1:1).

The ancient inhabitants to whom Moroni referred, and the Olmecs, the mother civilization of the Americas, appear to be the same people. A group of people that we have come to know as the Jaredites left the great tower at the time of the confusion of languages sometime during the third millennium BC, and were led by the Lord to a land which was "choice above all the lands of the earth" (Ether 1:42). The Lord said, "There shall be none greater than the nation which I will raise up unto me of thy seed, upon the face of the earth" (Ether 1:43). They lived in an area that Moroni called "this north country." The Olmec homeland is also referred to as the north country.

Ixtlilxochitl, a sixteenth-century Mesoamerican historian, also wrote in his history of a group of people who came from the great tower. They were led to a good and fertile land—today called Mexico. They lived in an area along the Gulf Coast.

Because of the marked similarities between the account of Moroni, the archaeological history of the Olmecs, and the account of Ixtlilxochitl, there is reason to believe that the accounts of all three sources refer to the same people.

The three sources above—the witnesses of archaeology, ancient history, and the Book of Mormon—

(Previous Page)
El Tajin is located in the State of Veracruz, about 200 miles north of Tres Zapotes, an abandoned Olmec site, and 100 miles from Teotihuacan. It was a city that was established towards the end of Book of Mormon history, and may have formed an alliance with Teotihuacan toward the end of that century. As proposed earlier, it is Teotihuacan that appears to have caused the downfall of the Nephite nation, a nation within the ancient Jaredite/Olmec territory.

(Right)
This mural shows two figures arrayed in royal attire. The top figure is speaking, which may suggest a superior role to the bottom figure, who is wearing a quetzal headdress. It might also portray a higher figure in the act of transferring kingship or authority to a lower figure.

testify that the final destruction of the Olmec/Jaredite people occurred about 300 BC and was extremely violent. Among the remains of this civilization are thirty large stone heads, which were discovered along the Gulf of Mexico.

Following the demise of the Jaredite/Olmec nation, the people became subjected to rulers from both the south and the north. The leading power in the land northward was Teotihuacan, who, along with Tikal, played a major role in the downfall of the Nephite nation. El Tajin is representative of many cities that developed around AD 300, and also may have formed an alliance with Teotihuacan at the time of the Nephite demise at AD 385.

(Left)
The central building of El Tajín is adorned with 365 niches, representing the days of the solar year. The ruins of El Tajín date from AD 300, corresponding with the Mayan Classic period and the apostasy period of the Book of Mormon. The Book of Mormon explains this time period as follows: "And they did still continue to build up churches unto themselves, and adorn them with all manner of precious things. And thus did two hundred and fifty years pass away. . . . And it came to pass that after three hundred and five years had passed away, (and the people did still remain in wickedness) Amos died; and his brother, Ammaron, did keep the record in his stead" (4 Nephi 1:41, 47).

(Above and Right)

All three witnesses, that is, archaeology, Ixtlilxochitl, and the Book of Mormon, refer to the first known civilization in Mesoamerica as large—giants. When members of Limhi's expedition in 121 BC discovered the remains of the ancient Jaredites, they noted the extraordinary size of some of the artifacts: "And behold . . . they have brought breastplates, which are large . . ." (Mosiah 8:10). The colossal stone heads carved from basalt are representative of the large race of people about whom Moroni wrote, "They were large and mighty men as to the strength of men" (Ether 15:26).

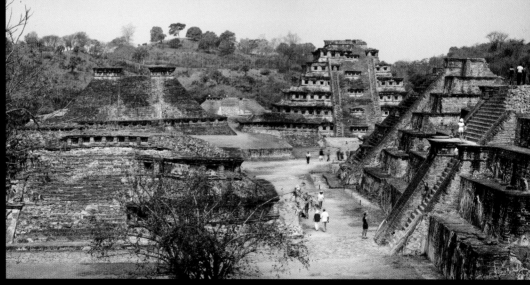

(Previous Page)
The people of El Tajin are referred to as the Totonac. The Totonac people, like their neighbors to the south, the Mayans, held a strong belief in the life hereafter. As a result, burial places and burial rights played a major role in their culture. The cemetery shown here is located at the base of a mountain where the tombs are built above ground. The concept of the resurrection was embedded in the hearts and minds of the people and continues to exist today. Although Catholicism introduced many new Christian principles, the traditional beliefs of the people already included a resurrection.

(Top-left, bottom-left, top-right)

These pictures represent the connection between two distinctly unique cultures that existed in the same general area. The Olmecs are best known for large, stone head figures and date from 1500 to 300 BC. The Totonac culture of El Tajin comprises the descendants of the Olmecs and new people who entered the area from the Mexico valley following the demise of the Olmec nation. These three structures (upper-right, upper-left, bottom-left) are related to the latter time period but still illustrate the themes developed by the earlier culture. For example, the movement of the yearly calendar is represented in the number of steps (upper-left) and the niches in the buildings (lower-left). The serpent motif is purposely designed into the later buildings like those at Mitla during the late Classic and early Postclassic periods (upper-right).

(Right and Above-center)

Major Olmec (Jaredite) sites included such places as Tres Zapotes and San Lorenzo, located in the State of Veracruz, and La Venta, located in the State of Tabasco. The following statement from the Book of Mormon may be referring to the Olmec site of La Venta: "And they built a great city by the narrow neck of land, by the place where the sea divides the land. . . . And the whole face of the land northward was covered with inhabitants" (Ether 10:20–21).

(Above)
Figure whose tongue is protruding in the same manner as the Aztec Calendar or Sun Stone. The portrayal of the sun traveling over the earth is a common Mesoamerican theme.

(Right)
There are five major sections at the archaeological sections at El Tajin. The most imposing structure is the Temple of the Niches. Three hundred sixty-five niches are carved into the building, representing the number of days of the year. The picture on the right shows a close-up of the Temple of the Niches. Although about 150 buildings have been identified at El Tajin, only twenty have been restored. Originally the area covered almost 1000 acres and boasted a population of about 30,000 people at its height. Its downfall occurred around AD 1100. Like many other sites throughout Mesoamerica, El Tajin could not support the costly hierarchy of priests in their culture.

SOUTHERN MEXICO

It may well be stated that no other places of antiquity in Mesoamerica have sparked the imagination of artists and scholars, poets and historians, casual visitors and sophisticated travelers as have the ancient Mayan archaeological ruins of Palenque, Chiapas, Mexico.

The name *Palenque*, with its less than glamorous interpretation "bone," is situated between the mountains of Chiapas and Lacandone to the south and the water-saturated land to the north whose ancient rivers drain into a place "where the sea divides the land"—today called the Gulf of Mexico.

Palenque is the geographical dividing region between two cultures, the Olmecs and the Mayans—or from a Book of Mormon perspective, the area between the Jaredites and the Nephites. Its historical timeline divides the Mayan Preclassic period (400 BC to AD 250) from the Classic period (AD 250–800), or, in Book of Mormon terms, the period covering Jarom to 4 Nephi, from Mormon to Moroni and beyond. Palenque endured as a major city for 600 years.

The inscriptions engraved on the walls of the tombs and on pottery vessels at Palenque record a dynasty consisting of thirty-four rulers beginning with Kúk' Bálam I (Quetzal Bird-Jaguar), who ascended to the throne on August 9, AD 435, and ending with Janaab' Pakal III, whose accession began on November 13, AD 799.

The elaborate tomb of K'nich Janaab Pacal I (Great-Sun-Shield), who was born on March 23, AD 603 and died on August 28, AD 683 at the age of 80, was uncovered by the great Mexican archaeologist Alberto Ruz Lhuillier. Although many tombs have been discovered in Mesoamerica since that time, the opening of Pacal's tomb stands as one of the most monumental events in the archaeology of the New World.

The contribution of Palenque to an understanding of the history of Mesoamerica is impressive. The English artist Fredrick Catherwood, who accompanied the explorer and writer John Lloyd Stephens to Palenque in 1839, exposed to the world and to the LDS Church an ancient civilization in the New World. Upon reading Stephens's book, some early leaders of the Church at Nauvoo suggested that perhaps Palenque was one of the ancient cities referred to in the Book of Mormon.

The dynastic and constructional time period of Palenque precludes it from being a major Book of Mormon city. Nevertheless, the fact that the Mayan Classic period (beginning at AD 250) is contemporary with the final years of Nephite history, and the fact that the Mayan Classic period was built on the foundation of the late Preclassic (400 BC to AD 250) Book of Mormon period, allow for some rather detailed comparisons.

(Previous Page)
The beginning of the Mayan Classic period, as represented at Palenque, correlates with the same time period as the Nephite apostasy recorded in 4 Nephi: "The people did harden their hearts, for they were led by many priests and false prophets to build up many churches, and to do all manner of iniquity" (4 Nephi 1:34). This is referring to the Mayan priests who, beginning in the third century AD, dressed in elaborate clothing and literally controlled the social, religious, and economic lives of the people. A gruesome ritualistic ceremony called blood-letting was practiced by these false prophets to demonstrate their role as leaders.

(Right)
The name "Mormon," as determined through comparisons in the Mayan language and the Book of Mormon, could be rendered in Mayan as "Jaguar of the Mountains." Mormon was a contemporary of the grandfather of Kuk Baalam (Quetzal-Jaguar), who is mentioned in the text. In the year AD 322, Mormon, who lived in the ancient Jaredite/Olmec territory (land northward), may have visited Palenque as well as other places such as Becan, El Mirador, and Tikal. He wrote, "And it came to pass that I, being eleven years old, was carried by my father into the land southward, even to the land of Zarahemla. The whole face of the land had become covered with buildings" (Mormon 1:6–7).

(Left and Above)

The corridor in the Palace of Palenque (left) shows the deterioration of the site, which was abandoned about AD 800. The Temple of the Inscriptions, now called the Tomb of Kinich Pakal Na, can be seen in the background. The figure (above) represents two Mayan figures, one in obeisance to the other. The larger figure is wearing a quetzal bird headdress, and inscriptions are shown in the upper-left portion of the picture. The archaeological ruins of Palenque have inspired many epigraphers, archaeologists, and linguists over the last 150 years. Artist Frederick Catherwood painted the ruins of Palenque in 1839–40, archaeologist Alberto Ruz discovered and excavated the tomb of Pacal in 1949–52, and art historian Linda Schele utilized the hieroglyphs at Palenque in her pioneer work in assisting others in deciphering the Mayan writing system.

(Left)
The breaking of the Mayan hieroglyphic code was greatly influenced by the detailed engravings at Palenque. Each engraved glyph represents a word or idea, and the Palenque glyphs were used to help decode the Mayan hieroglyphic system. Not displayed here, but similar in appearance to those shown right, is a glyph of interest to LDS scholars. When interpreted, it is the word Ut-chi. This literally means "and then it came to pass," a phrase that is used over 1,200 times in the Book of Mormon, serving as both event and date indicators.

(Above and Right)
The tomb of Pacal was discovered in 1949 when workmen noticed a thin break in the room at the top of the Pyramid of Pacal, which was engraved with inscriptions. After three years of laborious effort, the excavators under the direction of Dr. Alberto Ruz located the tomb. Before its discovery, no one considered these ancient pyramids to be burial tombs. Today it is common practice to search for burial tombs in any Mesoamerican excavation. The tombs help reveal the legacy of the Mayan kings.

Mayan images decorate the walls of the ancient ruins of Palenque and other Classic period (AD 250–800) sites. The dynasty at Palenque lasted thirteen generations. The top-left picture illustrates a ball game played with a large rubber ball. This ritualistic game appears to directly represent the art of warfare. The concept of kingship (middle-top) is emphasized by exquisite apparel. Hieroglyphs with the animal name of the individual (bottom-left) were common among the Mayans. The unification of the Olmec and Mayan civilizations (symbolically captured bottom-right) emphasizes the evolution of culture among the ancient Mayans. The top-right foliated niche from the Palace of Palenque is utilized by the Mayan epigraphers and is highlighted at the Temple of the Foliated Cross.

(Left)

Information taken from the Temple of the Cross at Palenque indicates that the son of Pacal, whose name is K'nich Kan Bálam II (Great-Sun-Snake-Jaguar) ascended to the throne on January 7, AD 684. He traced his genealogy to the ancient Jaredite/Olmec King Kish (U' Kish Kan). According to the panel of inscriptions at the Temple of the Cross, Kish was born on March 8, 993 BC and ascended to the throne in 967 BC.

(Above)

Mayan royalty began about AD 350 at Palenque, the same time that a priestcraft society began to control the social, religious, and commercial activities of the people in both the Book of Mormon and Mayan history. The manner of dress, the facial characteristics, and the arm positions all point to the careful artistry of those who formed the Mayan figures discovered on the walls of the Palace at Palenque.

(Above)

The bust of Chan (Kan) Baalam dates to the seventh century AD. A son of Pacal, he manifests the same facial features as can be seen today among the Mayans in Chiapas, Mexico.

(Right)

The representation to the right is of an individual adorned with a turquoise mask, jade necklaces, and pearl earrings, all of which were common burial items of the Mayan kings. The Book of Mormon refers to the late Preclassic and early Classic Mayan period wherein it states that the priests wore elaborate clothing, including pearls, and that they developed a class hierarchy (4 Nephi 1:24).

SOUTHERN YUCATAN PENINSULA

(Edzna, Becan, Chicanna, Kohunlich)

In the middle of the first century BC, many

located in the state of Campeche, Mexico, were built in the first century BC and provide an extraordinary visual representation of Moroni's defensive earthwork fortifications. If the historical assessment is accurate, then it was in this area where many cities were built, many wars were fought, many missionaries preached the gospel of Christ, a temple was built, and the Savior appeared to the Nephites.

(Previous Page)
The Mayan ruins of Edzna are located about 100 miles northwest of Becan, as the crow flies. The area's first permanent residents entered the valley around 400 BC, having migrated from the Peten region of Guatemala. Between 250 BC and AD 150 (Omni to 4 Nephi time period), Edzna underwent a period of phenomenal growth wherein thousands of people entered the region. They constructed a massive irrigation system with aqueducts extending as far as twelve kilometers from the center of the city. Like Becan, Edzna also had a defensive earthwork fortification built around the city.

(Left)
The photographer captures the shadows of this building at Edzna. The building is directly oriented to both the rising and setting of the sun. Located in the great acropolis near the Temple of Five Stores, this structure dates to around AD 700.

(Right)
Structure Fourteen or Temple of the Masks at Edzna, Campeche, houses two stucco masks, one of which is this magnificently detailed mask on the right. Dating to AD 600–750, this mask of a Classic period ruler is decorated to the hilt with penetrating eyes, a massive headdress, and symbols relating to the sun god. This representation suggests that it is the portrait of the ruler associated with the order of the solar deity.

(Left)
The word *becan* in the Mayan language means the "Path of the Serpent" and is reflected at the archaeological ruins of Becan by a serpentine path around the fortified city. The fortified earthworks at Becan were built in the middle of the first century BC, roughly Moroni's time period. The serpent motif has long been associated with deity in Mesoamerica. Therefore, it appears that the name Becan carries a double meaning. Just as the serpent around the city protects the people from their physical enemies, so does the deity serpent, like the staff of Moses, crush or destroy that old serpent, the enemy of all mankind, Satan. (See Helaman 8:13–15.)

(Left)

Beyond the remains of the ancient manmade trench fortifications at Becan is one of its major plazas. Ropes are used to assist the climber to the top of the twin-towered structure. From the top of the structure, the ancient city of Ixpujil can be seen, along with the sister city of Chicanna. About thirty miles southwest of Becan are the ruins of Calakmul, located in the largest biosphere reserve in Mexico. A massive civilization, much larger than exists in the same region today, occupied the landscape around Becan from 300 BC to AD 800. The history of the Book of Mormon encompasses 700 years of that 1,100-year time span.

(Above)

Over 200 buildings have been identified at Kohunlich. When combined with ruins from its immediate neighbor to the north, Dzibanche, this area is indicative of a huge population center dating from 100 BC to AD 800. The former cities are in a lush agricultural zone, situated in such a way that the heavens release a misty rain throughout the year, thus enabling crops to be harvested year-round. Because of its location, along with other archaeological and geographical data, this area represents a candidate for the land Bountiful, where a temple was built shortly after 35 BC.

Kohunlich is noted for its famous Kinich Ahau Mask (Lord of the Sun), which dates from the Nephite apostasy and Mayan Classic period.

(Top-right)
The limestone soil in the entire Yucatan region is not conducive to agricultural productivity. The tree roots spread along the surface or wrap themselves around each other in search of water. (See also picture on page 71.)

(Bottom-left)
This stone stele is called a *tun,* which is a Mayan word for "year." This is a concept initiated by the Mayans wherein a stone or tun would mark the passing of each year.

(Above-left, Above-center, Bottom-right)

Some of the most amazing and intricate artistic representations in all Mesoamerica exist along the southern Yucatan Peninsula, bordering Belize and Guatemala. The similar colored masks discovered at Kohunlich, Becan, and Edzna and other locations from the early Classic period (AD 250–400) strengthen the belief that these sites held close cultural ties. All the masks portrayed here bear the common theme of the sun god Kinich Ahau. *Kin* in the Mayan language means "sun" and signifies the day. *Ahau* means "lord" or "ruler."

Originally six masks were located at Kohunlich. One of the masks has since been looted. Although there are marked differences among the masks, they are all elaborately adorned with similar ornaments and engraved supporting headdresses. All manifest penetrating eyes, rounded facial features, thick lips, and rather large noses. The top-left mask features an Asiatic look common to the Olmec culture. The round facial features of the top-center and bottom-right masks also refelect the ancient Olmec culture. It is not uncommon for Mayan hierarchy to tie in their genealogy with Olmec kingship, as is the case at Palenque, where the seventh-century AD Mayan Chan Bálam traces his lineage to the tenth-century BC Olmec Kish Kan.

(Above)

The Mayan ruins of Chicanna are located just across the highway from Becan and 50 miles north of the Guatemalan border. Chicanna is representative of many other cities in this region that began to flourish in the middle of the first century BC. However, it was during the great Nephite apostasy period (AD 200—400) that the greatest growth and elaborate building construction occurred at Chicanna. Mormon describes the building structures dating to this period: "They did . . . adorn them with all manner of precious things" (4 Nephi 1:41).

(Right)

The flora of Mesoamerica adds to the rich cultural, historical, archaeological, and natural milieu.

NORTHERN YUCATAN PENINSULA

(Chichen Itza, Uxmal, Labnah, Tulum)

It has been variously reported that in all of America's past no figure is more exciting or more frustrating than that of the feathered serpent god Quetzalcoatl. It was said he was born of a virgin; was dressed in a white, flowing robe; was creator of the universe, god of the rain and the wind, author of baptism and the law of the fast; suffered death and came back to life; sailed off on a raft of serpents; and promised to return.

Latter-day Saints have often considered that the white god Quetzalcoatl and Jesus Christ are the same person and that the many archaeological sites located in the Northern Yucatan Peninsula were built by the Nephites. However, when associated with the Mayan archaeological ruins of Chichen Itza, Uxmal, Labnah, and Tulum, both of the above statements are false.

Although there may be links with the white god tradition and Christ, in relation to his visit to the Nephites, it is not reflected in the temple of Kukulcan at Chichen Itza. Kukulcan is a Mayan word that means the same as the Aztec word Quetzalcoatl. Both mean "beautiful bird-serpent."

Chichen Itza was settled about AD 500 as a Mayan city, almost one hundred years after the close of the Book of Mormon, and one hundred fifty years from the time the Nephites were driven out of the land southward or southward of the isthmus of Tehuantepec (proposed narrow neck of land). We know this from the treaty reported by Mormon that is recorded in Mormon 2:28–29:

> And in the three hundred and fiftieth year we made a treaty.... The Lamanites did give unto us the land northward, yea, even to the narrow passage which led into the land southward. And we did give unto the Lamanites all the land southward.

Around AD 1000 a political force from the distant valley of Mexico entered the northern Yucatan region and settled at Chichen Itza. For the next 200 years the Toltec style of architecture dominated that site.

Although the name Quetzalcoatl may have had its origin in the visit of Christ to the Nephites, many other priests took upon themselves the name of the deity Quetzalcoatl. One such individual is the tenth-century priest-warrior Topiltzin Quetzalcoatl, who came from the ancient and distant Toltec city of Tula. History reports that Topiltzin Quetzalcoatl was born in the year

AD 935 and left, or was driven out of, the Mexico valley and subsequently settled at Chichen Itza. Upon his arrival, this Mayan city was converted to a Toltec city.

The many serpent motifs visible at Chichen Itza and other post–Book of Mormon archaeological sites in the Northern Yucatan Peninsula either reflect a pagan and corrupt version of the white god Quetzalcoatl (Kukulcan) or are directly related to another individual who took upon himself the name of the deity. In historical legend the two concepts become confused.

(Above)

The ring on the side of the largest ball court yet discovered in Mesoamerica is located at the twelfth-century AD ruins of Chichen Itza. The game is of long duration, and debate continues regarding its origin, rules, and purpose. The walls of the ball court at Chichen Itza, along with engravings on vases and codices, provide details. It has been determined that the ball was round and consisted of a hard, rubber substance. The players wore protective gear over their legs and arms, and two teams battled each other. Stone rings visible on some Classic period sites suggest the concept of a goal.

(Right)

The obsession with the serpent concept is taken to the extreme at Chichen Itza. In this scene it is as if the serpents are guarding the entrance to the building. The serpent theme is dualistic in nature. If the serpent supports one's cause, then it is a physical deterrent against one's enemies. From a spiritual perspective, it is the deities (Kukulcan/Quetzalcoatl) who held the spiritual powers to provide eternal life. The Book of Mormon portrays the serpent as a type of the Messiah, comparing it to Moses' brazen serpent lifted up in the wilderness (Helaman 8:13–14).

(Left)
The Kukulcan Temple at Chichen Itza, although Toltec in style, has become a Mayan icon. It was built on top of a Mayan temple, and during the spring equinox, as the sun dips into the west, the shadows give the appearance that the serpent is moving or coming back to life. Thus the Temple of Kukulcan is dedicated to a tenth-century Quetzalcoatl (Kukulcan), and the powerful serpent motif ties him to the eternities. The rain god or hooked nose images are clearly visible in the foreground.

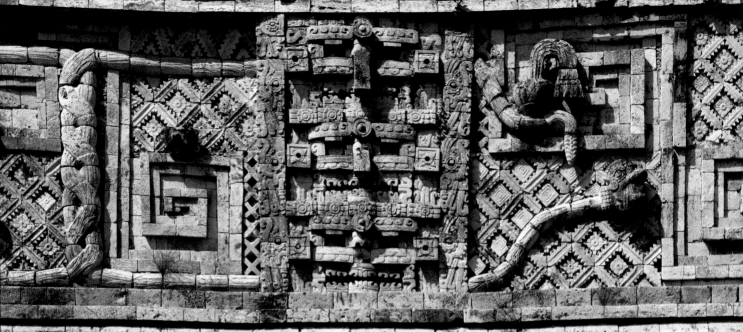

(Above and Right)

These two photographs illustrate the architectural and artistic ability of the Mayans from AD 400 to 900. In 1941, the explorer John Lloyd Stephens and his artist Frederick Catherwood spent several weeks at the site. Catherwood contracted a severe fever that almost took his life. Nevertheless, his drawings brought to life the antiquity of Mesoamerica and in the process labeled Stephens as the father of Mesoamerican archaeology.

(Top-right)
Named by Catholic scholars the "Quadrangle of the Nunnery," these elaborately adorned buildings at Uxmal surround a large courtyard. Of interest is that the architectural structure of the rooms was copied by the working population as a model for their homes, a style that still exists today. Uxmal was abandoned around AD 900.

(Bottom-right)
The small book of 4 Nephi ends with the date AD 320 and describes the elaborate dress of the false priests and elaborate apostate adornment of buildings. The Mayan post—Book of Mormon buildings at Uxmal and Kabah exhibit elaborate adornment to the extreme. It appears that the founding ruler of the dynasty of Uxmal was Hun-Utizil-Chac (First-Hill-Rain), whose name means "first Mayan priest who lived in the hills of Uxmal and who took upon himself the name of the rain god deity, Quetzalcoatl." These post—Book of Mormon lords, or priest-rulers, controlled the religious, social, and economic activities of the people for several centuries.

(Left)

The photographer captures the mystical beauty of the Governor's Palace at Uxmal. This ancient ruin's walls surround a great plaza. At the height of the land's occupation around AD 600, an apostate hierarchy ruled and commissioned many artists to create luxurious buildings. For the most part, the buildings served no practical purposes but were built at the mandate of the "many priests and false prophets" (1 Nephi 1:34). As early as AD 250, at the beginning of the apostate period, "the more wicked part of the people did wax strong," and they far outnumbered the people of God (4 Nephi 1:40).

(Above)

Book of Mormon Mayan ruins of Uxmal, like their neighbors, have traditionally portrayed the rain god Chac. New evidence suggests that the buildings at Uxmal were not dedicated to the rain god. Rather, just as Tolpiltizin Quetzacacoatl at Chichen Itza was named after the deity Quetzalcoatl, so at Uxmal was Lord Chac named after the rain god deity whose name is also associated with Quetzalcoatl. The sixteenth-century Mexican writer Alva de Ixtlilxochitl wrote that the deity Quetzalcoatl was also called the God of Rains and the Tree of Life.

(Previous Page)
The temple of Kukulcan was called "El Castillo" (The Castle) by the first bishop of the Yucatan, Diego de Landa. It is strategically located between the platform of the warriors and the ball court. Today there is an ongoing debate about the origin of the Toltec structures at Chichen Itza. Traditionally, the rulers of the later period of Chichen Itza were reported to have come from Mexico. Some new literature proposes that the builders were people who migrated up the east coast and were Mayanized Mexicans under the domination of the Mexican Toltecs. The Temple of Kukulcan was built on top of a Mayan architectural structure that proudly displayed a red jaguar monument at its zenith.

(Above and Right)
When the original serious excavation work began at Chichen Itza under the direction of noted archaeologist Sylvanias Morley, the Mayans were considered a peace-loving people. This concept was quickly abandoned. The Palace of the Skulls is located near the ball court, a place where the Mayans appear to have reenacted battles. The "enemies" were decapitated whether they lost the game or not. This idea of displaying the skulls of the enemies continued into the sixteenth century AD at Tenochtitlan (Mexico City).

Chris Parkinson

OTHER REGIONS

And it came to pass that there were many who died,

firmly believing that their souls were redeemed by the Lord

Jesus Christ; thus they went out of the world rejoicing.

And there were some who died with fevers, which

with the rainy season. Fevers and diseases come naturally during the rainy season (May through October)—brought on by a mosquito that brings both sickness and death. But the wonderful thing about it is that God has also provided excellent qualities of plants and roots in that same rain forest to counteract the temporal sickness and death.

Regarding the archaeological site of Tikal, there is good evidence to suggest that it may have been one of the cities in the east wilderness of Zarahemla that was established or expanded by Moroni, his army, and the Nephites in the first century BC. "And it came to pass that Moroni caused that his armies should go forth into the east wilderness; yea, and they went forth and drove all the Lamanites who were in the east wilderness into their own lands, which were south of the land of Zarahemla" (Alma 50:7).

Although Tikal was occupied as early as 600 BC, it was in 72 BC that "many cities" were built by the Nephites and that Tikal manifested an increase in population. It is also during this same time period when not only Tikal but other places became strongholds as a result of defensive earthworks built around the city.

However, the most significant relationship with Tikal and the Book of Mormon occurred in the year AD 378, when the dictator from Teotihuacan, "Spear Thrower Owl," sent his young son with a powerful army to capture Tikal and take control of the Peten region. It is in this environment wherein the combined forces of Teotihuacan and Tikal completely annihilate the Nephites as related in the writings of Mormon: "I, Mormon, began to be old; and knowing it to be the last struggle of my people . . ." (Mormon 6:6; see Mormon 6:1–5).

(Previous Page)
This section introduces some of the most poignant photography available regarding two major regions of ancient America: Tikal, Guatemala, and Machu Picchu, Peru. Although separated by distance, time, and culture, both Tikal and Machu Picchu evoke deep emotional feelings within the modern visitor. Machu Picchu, along with Chichen Itza, has been named one of the Seven Wonders of the World, and Tikal has the distinction of being labeled a Heritage for Humanity from both a historical and naturalistic point of view. This particular photograph depicts Peruvian architecture in the fourteenth to sixteenth centuries.

(Right)
Tikal is located in Guatemala's Peten region and borders Belize on the east and Mexico on the north and west. Tikal served as a city center for over fourteen hundred years from 600 BC to AD 800. It reached its population zenith around AD 600, a date which correlates with the structure labeled Temple Two shown on the right. It has been estimated that the population of Tikal reached about 60,000–100,000 during the period described above. Tikal's Preclassic era (Book of Mormon time period) is contemporary with the great acropolis region of El Mirador to the north and Cancuen to the south.

(Above and Center-right)
Revealed to the English-speaking world by Yale University Professor Hiram Bingham in 1911, Machu Picchu had been abandoned for over two hundred years. Initially it was thought that Machu Picchu was mysteriously built during the time of the Spanish conquest. It now appears that it was built as a place of refuge in the fifteenth century. Its breathtaking view allows one to see the rising and setting of the sun from the citadel—in spite of the high mountain peaks. The buildings above and to the right were constructed from large, airtight

(Above-right)
A Lacandone Indian dressed in white robes with his small son by his side selling bows and arrows to tourists who visit the site of Palenque, Chiapas, Mexico. The Lacandone, a small group of people, have lived for centuries near the Usumacinta River and near the archaeological site of Bonampak. Although there is no such thing as a white Lamanite, some early Latter-day Saint literature proposed the Lacandones to be white Lamanites, a myth that originated with their traditional white robes. Today only about three hundred Lacandone still live in the jungle regions of

(Immediate right)
Water flows freely from what is labeled the Princess Sacred Fountain or Royal Bath Houses. It is difficult to image a more serene and beautiful setting. The unique workmanship of stoneworks, along with the water systems, produce a breathtaking landscape.

© Chris Parkinson

© Chris Parkinson

© Chris Parkinson

(Bottom-center and Bottom-right)
The visitor can take a one-day trek from Cuzco by train to the base of the mountains and then by bus as the road winds its way up to the top of the paradisiacal setting of Machu Picchu. The first glimpse of the ancient city is an emotional experience for many. Some hike into the ruins in order to drink in more of the flavor of this incredible site. The Inca people of today are small in stature and friendly by nature. Vending booths with fresh fruit are common in both the Mexican and Peruvian cultures.

(Above Far-right)
A curved-wall structure called the Temple of Sun houses what is considered to be a sacred stone. Located high on the mountaintops, the temple is built in such a way as to allow the sun to cast its rays inside the temple over the sacred stone during the early morning hours of the summer solstice. Although the Incas did not have a standardized written language, they had the ability to accomplish phenomenal building feats, creating structures that took into account the celestial events of the sun, moon, and stars.

(Left)

Over 1,500 buildings have been identified at Tikal dating from 600 BC to AD 800, including Temples 1–5, the Lost World, and the North Acropolis. The construction of these temples and burial tombs was a heavy financial drain on the native ancestral populace, and their societies became top heavy, which may have contributed to the nation's demise. This picture shows the west side of Temple Two and measures 125 feet high. It was common practice to place a stone (tun) in front of the pyramid, accompanied by a circular altar to recognize the ruler associated with the pyramid.

(Above)

This round, engraved stone dates to approximately AD 711 and depicts two Mayan figures dressed in royal attire. One figure is identified as Jasaw Chan Kawii (AD 682–734). Surrounding the two figures are glyphs which provide genealogical and historical information. Originally it was thought that the engravings were purely pictorial in nature. During the last twenty-five years, it has been determined that they are also phonetic, and the Mayan code began to be deciphered, thus allowing a more complete understanding of the people whose history is engraved upon the stones.

(Previous Page)
The photographer captures the essence of Machu Picchu. The stonework of the Temple of the Sun and the regal mountains in the background create the haunting shadow of a city that has been abandoned for over 500 years—since about the time of the conquest of Peru. The traditions of Machu Picchu and Peru, however, still exist. The legends of a white god named Viracocha are etched in the minds of the Incas today just as their ancient history is etched in stone.

(Left)
This photograph was taken from atop the largest pyramid of Tikal, labeled Temple Four. This pyramid towers 212 feet above the jungle floor and appears to be associated with Lord Yikin Chan Kawiil, who ascended to the throne December 8, AD 734. The interior of the temple consists of small chambers, a direct contrast to the large, imposing exterior. Excavation work at Tikal was initially conducted by the University of Pennsylvania and is currently proceeding under the direction of the Guatemala Institute of Archaeology. These excavations have contributed a detailed understanding of this once-great Mayan city located in one of the immense jungles of the world.

(Above)
A combination of nature in an unparalleled setting and man's accomplishments and failures is portrayed in this poetic scene from a once-great city that now lies in ruins. Occupation at Tikal began as early as 600 BC, and by the end of the ninth century AD all vestiges of royal power had ceased. Like its neighbors in the Mayan world, the city center surrendered its elite quarters to squatters. The new inhabitants built thatched homes among the ruins, where some pursued the buried tomb treasures of the glorious past. By the eleventh century AD, the 1,500 buildings of Tikal were left in ruins, to be choked out by the roots and vines of nature. Almost 800 years would pass before modern civilization took a look at this once mighty fortified city-state.

(Left)

These stone monuments in front of a building at Tikal were used to mark each year. The concept of marking time on a yearly basis was a common theme among Mayan scribes as well as the Book of Mormon writers. Mormon wrote, "And thus did pass away the ninety and sixth year; and also the ninety and seventh year; and also the ninety and eighth year; and also the ninety and ninth year; and also an hundred years had passed away since the days of Mosiah, who was king over the people of the Nephites" (3 Nephi 2:4—5).

(Above)
This tropical flowering plant from Peten, Guatemala, is typical of the variety of beautiful flowers found in the National Park of Tikal. Because this area has been established as a nature reserve, it beckons visitors to Tikal with not only ancient history but also the beauty of this mysterious region of the world.

(Right)
These steps conceal the entrance to what is called the "royal tomb" at Machu Picchu. Despite its name, no bones or tombs have been discovered in this cavelike structure, but inside the "tomb" is a stepped altar along with several niches positioned to capture the early morning rays of the sun. Such Inca stone masonry is represented not only at Machu Picchu, but also in many other places throughout the immense Inca kingdom.

N

El Tajin

Teotihuacan

MEXICO CITY

Veracruz

ACAPULCO

MEXICO

PACIFIC OCEAN

MESOAMERICA

25 MILES   100 MILES   200 MILES